Education for Democracy in the 21st Century

Helen Osieja

Preface

The idea to write this book arose after my personal experiences as a teacher, citizen, researcher, and a short time as a political analyst in the Swedish Parliament. I realized that what was taught in school under the name of "democracy" did not reflect what politicians actually said and did.

I observed with great interest what was going on during the political campaign for the Swedish parliamentary elections of 2018. I found that many teachers did not teach their students critical thinking, respect for pluralism and tolerance. On the contrary, I saw how some teachers incited and indoctrinated students against parties they did not like and how the police on several occasions had to intervene to stop confrontations in front of the party booths.

I had an assignment at the Swedish parliament as a political analyst which unfortunately did not last long. The work itself was fascinating, but when I pointed out to a Member of Parliament that she used many terms incorrectly, it was enough for her to fire me. I realized that the MP had no education whatsoever in either political science or international law, even though she was responsible for issues relating to international relations and migration. These experiences of having seen examples of incompetence and opportunism made me first begin to doubt the value of democracy as a form of government. But I soon realized that the solution is not to dismantle democracy because of incompetent politicians; on the contrary, if democracy does not work as it should, it means that democracy must be enhanced.

As the events that unfolded on January 6, 2021 in Washington, D.C. prove, democracy is today in danger in many countries of the world precisely because of ignorance regarding the pillars and tenets of democracy. It is also in danger because of politicians who forget that they have been elected as public servants and that therefore it is their duty to serve the people, not to be served by the people. As British historian and politician Lord Acton wrote: "Power corrupts, and absolute power corrupts absolutely."

Acknowledgements

First of all, I would like to thank the Helge Axelsson Johnson's Foundation of Sweden for the grant that made the publication of this book possible. I would also like to thank my beloved husband, Jonny Kennet Persson, for his support and encouragement to write it. Morten Källström and Olle Felten, thank you for convincing me that it pays to fight for democracy. Professor Vinayagum Chinapah, thank you for your comments and suggestions for making this textbook more didactic. A special thank you to the Swedish parliament, which -somewhat surprisingly- has provided me with an example of how harmful hubris, incompetence, ignorance, and opportunism are for elected politicians.

Helen Osieja

Stockholm, January 2021.

Table of Contents

Introduction

The aim of this book is to prepare future citizens for living in a democratic country. To inform them about their rights and duties. To clarify that, while democracy implies freedom, it is not the same as anarchy, because rights go hand in hand with responsibilities. Unfortunately, the last decade has been characterized by an increasing polarization and political violence; dialogue has been substituted for by insults, labels, and other types of aggression.

While conflict in a society is healthy because it denotes the existence of pluralism, violence is not. Democracy, with all its flaws, is still much better than all other forms of government: No other form of government is characterized by a peaceful transfer of power; no other form of government allows its subjects the personal freedoms that we take for granted in democracies, and no other form of government makes rulers accountable for their actions.

It seems that many people have forgotten what the pillars of democracy are, and assume they have the right of attacking and harassing others only because they do not share their political views. Lamentably, bullying and harassment do not stay out of the workplace, and the author has experienced how not agreeing with the majority caused her to be bullied by colleagues and even excluded from a Christmas dinner. Other people fare much worse- they can even be beaten up for just not agreeing with what the majority thinks.

Demonstrations turn often into riots that produce multiple arrests. People get wounded at rallies that turn violent and, as some unfortunate cases prove, can even be killed.

This is a textbook for a basic course in democratic values. It is intended mainly for young people who will soon come of age and become citizens, as well as for immigrants from non-democratic countries that maybe do not know what rules apply in their new country of residence. The book covers content for 24 to 30 lesson hours. At the end of each lesson there is a glossary and questions that can be discussed in a group and others that can be answered as an assignment.

The first chapter presents what politics is about and discusses the factors of political struggle. It also explains the differences between democratic and other forms of government, like authoritarian, totalitarian and theocratic. It discusses the role of the citizen in politics and presents the aims of the course.

The second chapter explains the tenets of democracy and what these mean for the citizen. Furthermore, it discusses the rights and responsibilities of the citizen in a democracy.

The subject of the third chapter is political parties and ideologies. The chapter presents the main ideologies that exist in democratic systems nowadays, and the importance of ideologies that distinguish political parties. Furthermore, it presents the main differences between democratic and undemocratic political parties.

The fourth chapter discusses the characteristics of the ideal democratic society, like secularism, the strict division of political and civil society, - which is non-existent in other political systems-, the separation of the private and the public life realms, the significance of freedom of religion and the principle of the rule of law in a democracy.

The topic of the fifth chapter is democratic political culture: It defines political culture, discusses the role of the agents that form political culture in a society, the forging of national identity and the main components of a democratic political culture, which include, but are not limited to, the rule of law, the equality of all citizens before the law, and secularism.

The sixth chapter presents the enemies of democracy, that is, all attitudes, behaviors and organizations that directly or indirectly pose a threat to democracy.

The seventh chapter is the conclusion of the textbook, and it summarizes the rights and obligations of the citizen in a democracy.

Some concepts are mentioned in more than one chapter, because they are relevant in more than one way, like is the case of the rule of law. The rule of law is not only a basic tenet of all systems that call themselves democratic, but also a concept of political culture. The same is true of the equality of all citizens before the law.

This book is not, and does not intend to be, an advanced course on political science. Its aim, though, is to be a guide for course participants of what to expect from, and how to behave in a democracy.

1.   What is politics all about?

You might ask yourself why discuss politics at all if you are not interested in the subject. Yet, you live in a country with a political system and a social order. With laws, norms and regulations which you might agree or disagree with, <u>but which you must obey.</u>

Politics is about **public administration**, that is, <u>the management of the resources of the country.</u> Political leaders are the ones who decide how the limited resources of the country are to be used, and who is to benefit from those resources. As resources are limited and needs unlimited, there will be disagreement as to how to best use the economic resources of the state. But politics is also about **power,** or the capacity to influence others. Power can be economic, like is the case of enterprises which can influence politicians to pass laws favorable to their interests. Power can also be military, that is, the capacity of a country to use force to defend its interests. But power can also be based on knowledge, and that is why education is so important for the citizen. An educated citizen will be capable to defend her rights much better than an illiterate citizen, who is probably not even aware of what her leaders are doing.

In democracies, the struggle for power is carried out in elections, in which **political parties** compete for the votes of the citizens. Political parties are registered organizations with a minimum number of members which participate in elections. Political parties usually have an **ideology,** which is a system of opinions, of values and of beliefs. Political parties claim to represent the interests of particular groups of people. For example, in Sweden there is a feminist party which claims to represent the rights of women. Likewise, there are workers' parties in many countries which claim to represent the rights of the working classes. In any case, what must be kept in mind is that <u>the main aim of political parties is to gain votes in an election so they can obtain political power.</u>

1.1.   The factors of the political struggle

No matter how wealthy a country is, economic resources will always be limited while the needs of the people are unlimited. Since governments obtain their economic resources from taxes paid by the citizens, a main factor of struggle is socioeconomic, that is, how the resources will be used, and who will benefit from them. While for some people the struggle for political power is limited to the socioeconomic realm, most will admit that there are other relevant factors, like ideological, religious, national, racial, and cultural factors.

Since social and economic inequality exists in all countries, there are different social classes with different interests. While a businessman and a worker employed by him might be compatriots, one can expect that their perspectives and their interests are going to be different, and that they will most likely vote for different political parties.

Furthermore, since most countries have a diverse population, cultural factors play a role as well. In ethnically diverse countries, political parties might have a cultural profile representing a group of people. An example of this are parties with an ethnic or religious profile, which claim to represent people who belong to a given ethnic or religious group.

1.2.   The struggle for power in different political systems

As mentioned above, all countries or political entities have limited resources and unlimited needs. All countries or political entities have to face choices as to how the resources are used and who is going to benefit from those resources. In all political entities there will be individuals or groups that aim to attain power and influence others, but the ways the struggle for power looks like will vary greatly between democratic and non-democratic entities.

In democratic countries, the struggle is peaceful and takes place in the form of elections. The transfer of power from one political party or parties to other political parties takes place peacefully. In contrast, in non-democratic countries, the struggle is violent and is carried out as rebellions, riots or revolutions. Sometimes these rebellions or revolutions can last years and cost thousands of lives. The political struggle depends on which group can exert more violence on its opponents, and once in power the victors will forbid all competition for power. Since there is no legal opposition, the losers are forced to go underground, and their activities will be declared illegal by the group in power. In non-democracies there is no opposition, but rather dissidence. **Dissidents**, or people who disagree with the government, are often persecuted, arrested, put in jail and in some cases tortured or killed.

In democracies political parties promise positive changes and benefits to their electors. Electors choose the party they believe best represents them, and the contest is decided by the number of votes each party obtains in an election. If the **government** (the political party in power at a given moment in a **state**) does not deliver what it promised, it risks losing its electors to another party or parties. It is the people who decide which party or parties attain political power in a democracy, and parties respect their opponents in the political struggle.

In non-democratic countries, power is tantamount to physical violence and intimidation. People do not get to elect their representatives, and usually the only way to get rid of them is using violence as well.

1.3.   The citizen in politics

In democracies, politicians are called public servants, because they are elected by the people to serve them. If public servants do not deliver what they promised, or if they misbehave while in office, the people can demand their dismissal.

In contrast, in non-democracies politicians are served by the people. They do not represent the people of the country and they use the country's resources to satisfy their own needs, as there is nobody who will demand **accountability**.

As stated above, knowledge empowers people. An educated population will not permit abuses of power by the government; it will demand accountability and will express its will in elections by voting. Furthermore, an educated population will not be fooled and manipulated as easily as an illiterate population. An educated people will defend their rights, organize and protest -albeit in a peaceful manner- whenever they perceive that their leaders are not doing what is expected of them.

It is a very unfortunate fact that the poor, the most marginalized members of society, do not usually vote and therefore have little or no chance of improving their situation. It is easy for the powerful to take advantage of a population who does not know how to defend their rights.

You might think, but what can I as a private citizen do to influence my political leaders? Well, a lot, together with a group of people who share your interests and concerns. You can join an interest group. You can start a petition for something you consider important. You can join a political party and run for office. You can file a lawsuit against the government if you believe that you have been wronged by it and obtain a redress. But you can do this only if you are involved.

1.4.   Aims of this course

You live in a democracy because you were either born in one or you and your family decided to immigrate to a country with a democratic system. You have probably become a citizen either by becoming an adult (in most countries at 18 years of age) or by **naturalization**, that is, by obtaining the citizenship of a country other than your country of birth. Or you will soon come of age and be able to vote.

<u>The only path for a people or a country to flourish is peace</u>. In democracies, conflict is inevitable (like in any other system), but violence is not. Respecting differences and solving conflicts peacefully is indispensable to avoid violence not only at the national level, but also to preserve peace at the international level. Violence threatens democracy, stability, and peace.

Your classmates, colleagues, friends, and relatives might have opinions different from yours, but that does not make them despicable. Not in a democracy, because pluralism is one of its pillars. You might find it impossible to agree with certain people, but you can always agree to disagree without becoming enemies.

Democracy is a form of government where citizens have the right to live their lives in the way they choose. Democracy allows us to have our own opinions without being afraid of punishment. However, democracy is a fragile form of government because there are many forces which see it just as an instrument to attain power and not as an end in itself.

This course has several aims:

1. To prepare you to be a responsible citizen of a democratic country, and to assume the rights and responsibilities that living in a democracy implies.

2. To clarify what the limits to our rights in a democracy are, namely, the rights of other people, common good, and social order.

3. To prepare you to defend your opinions and your rights without breaking the law.

4. To clarify why conflict and violence are not synonyms, and that while conflict is inevitable and healthy, violence is only destructive.

Nonetheless, this book does not aim to convince you of any political ideology or of voting for any party, because that is something that <u>only you can decide</u>. Hopefully, this book can aid you in deciding what your political preferences are, and of motivating you to assume your rights and responsibilities as a citizen of a democratic country.

Naturalization ceremony in Florida, USA, 2012. These people have officially become US citizens.

Glossary

Accountability – The responsibility of a politician for the choices she makes on behalf of his or her people.

Dissident – A person who is critical of the government in non-democratic systems.

Government – The public administration of a state at a given period.

Ideology – A system of ideas, of opinions and beliefs not based on scientific evidence, and therefore not able to be proven true or false.

Naturalization – The process by which an alien can become a citizen of a country other than his or her country of birth.

Pluralism – The coexistence of different political ideologies, parties, and organizations in a country.

Political parties – The entities in a democracy which can directly participate in elections. An organization must usually have a minimum number of members to be considered a political party.

Power – The capacity to influence others without being influenced by them.

Public administration – the management of the state's affairs, for example the economy, the health system, and the educational system.

State – The institutions that rule over a territory and its people.

Topics for discussion:

1. Are you politically involved in any way? If the answer is NO, what issues could motivate you to become politically active?

2. Could you be a good friend of somebody who has totally different political opinions from your own? Why?

Questions:

1. What is public administration?

____

____

____

____

____

2. Give examples of
a) economic power

____

____

____

____

____

b) military power

____

____

____

____

____

c) power of knowledge

____

____

____

____

____

3. Name two political parties of your country of residence. What are their main differences?

____

____

____

____

____

4. Name three factors of political struggle.

____

____

____

____

____

5. What does the concept of **pluralism** mean?

____

____

____

____

____

6. How are conflicts solved in a democracy as compared to other forms of government?

____

____

____

____

____

2. You live in a democracy. What does this mean?

You probably like a politician or a candidate. You have probably decided to vote for her. Or maybe you have decided not to vote, because you do not like any candidate. It is your choice. However, you must understand that many people in the world -actually most people in the world- do not have the choices you do. Many people in the developing world may not vote. Or may not express their contempt for incompetent leaders, because they can face punishment that can go from imprisonment to death. Many people simply do not have a right to decide who they want to represent them. They just know who their leader is and that they are expected to obey that individual, no matter how corrupt or incompetent he may be. People in **authoritarian** or **totalitarian** regimes must accept the fact that they may be imprisoned for any reason at all, and that there are few or no instances to obtain help from if the imprisonment is wrong or unfair. They have no right to question the government or the actions that it takes- maybe an **illegitimate** government which might not represent its subjects at all; a government which instead of serving the people is served by its people.

Democratic governments, you might think, have many shortcomings. And it is true: There is **corruption, cronyism,** incompetence, inefficacy... But at least the people can decide who they want to have as leaders, who they want to represent them and their interests. And if the leaders do not perform their duties, vote them out of office or demand their resignation. Democracy is by no means a perfect form of government, but it is definitely better than other political systems.

2.1. What is democracy?

The Online Etymology Dictionary defines democracy as «government by the people, system of government in which the sovereign power is vested in the people as a whole, exercising power directly or by elected officials; a state so governed. » It comes from the Greek dēmokratia, which means « popular government » from *demos* (people) and *kratos* (rule, strength).

Democracy is a system of government that evolved in ancient Greece. Democracy was originally *direct,* that is, the men of Athens voted on initiatives directly in a public assembly. Today due to the size and complexity of most modern states, direct democracy is practiced in very few countries, one of them is Switzerland.

The citizens of ancient Greece voted using stones of different colors.

Most democracies are nowadays *indirect,* which means that the citizens elect the leaders that they think will best represent their interests in **parliament** or **congress**. Since citizens have different preferences, different values and priorities, there are at least 2 major political parties citizens can choose from, like is the case of the United States of America or the United Kingdom. In other democracies, like the Scandinavian countries, there are multiple political parties citizens can choose from, and many candidates within those parties. But what is most relevant in any democratic system is the fact that it is the **citizens** who vest power in their political representatives for a given period. If citizens are dissatisfied with the performance of the politicians they chose, they may choose another representative in a coming election, or even demand that the incompetent politician resign from her post.

But most importantly, democracy implies <u>the peaceful transfer of power</u> from one head of government to his or her successor. Unlike in authoritarian or totalitarian governments, there is no bloodshed, no violence or loss of life when a leader steps down to let the next elected leader assume power. After all, in a democracy it is the governed who decide who is going to rule them.

Democracy is associated with a way of life as well: In democracies citizens enjoy civil and political rights and freedoms. However, democracy does not imply that the citizen can do as she pleases because

Citizens of the United States of America voting in the 2016 election.

a pillar of democracy is <u>the rule of law</u>. Nobody can imprison a citizen for choosing to believe (or not to believe) in the tenets of a religion, or for expressing her opinion, in oral or written form. Of course, there are limits to the freedom of speech and the freedom of press. Slander and harassment are forbidden. But citizens may express their opinions without being afraid of legal consequences, as long as there is no calumny, harassment or incitement to violence.

Furthermore, <u>there is a strict division between the civil society and the political society</u>. An example of this division is the presence of all the non-governmental organizations (**NGOs)** that exist in democratic countries but are usually absent in countries with other forms of government. Examples of NGOs are human rights organizations, animal rights organizations, religious institutions and charities. Furthermore, in a democracy there are multiple religious institutions citizens may choose from because there is no official religion. <u>Religion and politics are totally separate realms in a secular democracy</u>.

And most importantly, there is **separation of powers** in a democracy. Politicians do not tell judges how to decide on a ruling, since courts (the **judiciary power**) are independent from the **executive** (the head of government and the ministers) or the **legislative power** (Parliament or congress, where law initiatives are voted by the people's representatives).

2.2. Democracy compared with other forms of government

As stated above, the main characteristic of democracy is **suffrage,** or regular elections. All citizens are entitled to one vote and have the right to choose whoever they feel is best suited to represent them. The losers of the election step down and the winners attain power in a peaceful process, the inauguration or transfer of power.

This is not the case in **authoritarian governments.** In non-democratic governments politicians are not elected by the people. In many cases, they have come to power using violence and intimidation and the transfer of power is all but peaceful. Military governments imprison those citizens who voice critical opinions. Imprisonment and torture are often consequences critical citizens face. In some cases, criticism of the regime can cost citizens their lives.

In authoritarian governments there is no contest for political power. Therefore, there is usually one political party, like in the case of the People's Republic of China. Citizens who disobey the rules imposed by the Chinese government may face imprisonment, torture or death. People may not express negative opinions about the government or read literature which is critical of the government.

A man brutally beaten in Hong Kong by the Chinese police. China has a totalitarian system of government that controls practically all aspects of the citizens' lives.

In an authoritarian government with no **pluralism** there is usually one **ideology**, one party, and obedience to whatever the authorities say.

There may be a market economy, though. People might be allowed to own and run a business as long as this does not represent any threat to the government. This is a difference between an authoritarian and a **totalitarian** government.

A **totalitarian government** is very much like an authoritarian government: a one-party system, no elections, no pluralism. Furthermore, in totalitarian governments, like North Korea, the government runs the economy. Citizens may not own businesses or any property. The government is the sole provider of goods and services, and citizens must accept them no matter how deficient these may be.

In a totalitarian system, the citizen's life is even more controlled by the government than in an authoritarian system of government. Leaders do not usually leave power until they die, and when they do it is normally passed to a relative or a close friend of the deceased leader. This practice is called **nepotism.**

Another type of government which exercises full control over its subjects' lives is a **theocracy.** This is probably the most oppressive form of government. In a theocracy, citizens do not have freedom of conscience. There is one official religion and the penalty for not following the tenets of that religion can go from corporal punishment to death. It does not matter if citizens do not believe in the official religion, they are forced to follow it in every aspect of their lives, since there is no division between public and private life.

An example of a theocracy is Saudi Arabia. In Saudi Arabia there is no constitution. The Quran, the sacred book of Islam, is considered the law of the country and is interpreted by clergymen. The people have no say on the laws that govern them, on whether these are current or maybe obsolete, and on how they lead their lives. Women in Saudi Arabia are not allowed to leave their homes without the permission of their guardian, who is a male member of the family. Women are not allowed to wear the clothes they like- they must cover themselves from head to toe with a hijab. And women are not allowed to marry whoever they choose. Marrying a foreigner is not legal for Saudi women.

2.3.   Rights and Responsibilities of a Citizen in a Democracy

In a democratic political system there is a constitution, or fundamental law, which contains a **bill of individual rights.** The aim of it is precisely to protect the citizen from abuses of power. This bill gives citizens certain rights, like freedom of speech, freedom of the press, freedom of religion, freedom of association, etc. These rights, called in some countries « individual guarantees » cannot usually be encroached upon by the state. The citizen has the empowerment to file a lawsuit against the state if these rights are not respected by the authorities, and to appeal if she is not satisfied with the ruling. Since in a democracy courts are independent of the legislative and the executive powers, the citizen and the state are treated like two equal parties in a dispute.

However, living in a democracy implies responsibilities for the citizen as well. Maybe the most important of these is respecting the **rule of law.** Citizens in a democracy have the obligation to respect the laws of their country, no matter whether they like them or not. For example, adults must pay taxes for the services which are provided by the state. Likewise, if a citizen is wronged by another citizen, he may not take justice into his own hands. In a democracy, the citizen has a right to demand justice in a peaceful manner, and to file a lawsuit against whoever wronged him. The citizen can appeal a decision he does not agree with, but not punish the wrongdoer personally. In any case, it is the state who provides for justice and not the citizens themselves. <u>It is punishable to take justice in one's own hands.</u>

Another obligation is respecting the rights of others, no matter how different the lifestyles of these people are. If say, a conservative family is against homosexuality and they have a son who is a homosexual, they have the obligation to respect the son's sexual orientation and his right to live his life according to his own wishes. Likewise, all citizens are obliged to respect the political views of other citizens, no matter how much they may dislike them.

In a democracy <u>all citizens are equal before the law</u>, and this means that men, women, racial minorities, homosexuals, etc. are treated in the same manner by the country's institutions. <u>It is of major importance to point out that non-citizens do not enjoy the same rights citizens have</u>. This applies for foreigners who do enjoy some protection granted by international human rights conventions and treaties, as well as for young people who are underage and for this reason are subjected to the authority of their parents or guardians.

Glossary

Authoritarian government- A government which does not allow opposition or criticism. Authoritarian governments are not usually elected by the people- rather, they take power by force.

Bill of rights- a charter of rights citizens enjoy and which can only be encroached upon by the government under extraordinary circumstances like war.

Citizen- adult subject of a country. Children are considered nationals but not citizens of a country, because they cannot vote.

Congress- Is the equivalent of parliament in presidential democracies.

Corruption- Lack of transparency and of accountability of political leaders. Also defined as the use of public funds for private purposes.

Cronyism- The practice of politicians of assigning political posts to their friends or relatives without regarding their qualifications.

Executive- the authority responsible of carrying out the laws approved by the legislative branch (Congress or Parliament.)

Ideology- A set of opinions and beliefs which conform a view of the world not based on facts but on subjective values. "Ready packages of thought".

Illegitimate government- a government that does not represent the interests of the people it rules.

Judiciary Power- the system of courts in a country where the law is interpreted.

Legislative Power- the authority responsible for creating laws- it is usually called congress in presidential democracies, and parliament in parliamentary democracies.

Nepotism- the act of giving positions of power to friends or relatives. Synonymous to cronyism.

NGO- non-governmental organization with a particular aim. Examples of NGOs are human rights organizations, environmental organizations, etc. which do not depend on the government to exercise their functions.

Parliament- In parliamentary democracies, the place where elected representatives of the people meet to debate and draft new laws. The legislative branch of government.

Rule of law- A political system where there is a clear separation of powers (legislative, executive and judicial) and where regulations apply to every subject, independently of who he or she is.

Separation of powers- means that law-making, law-enforcement and law interpretation are carried out by institutions independent of each other.

Suffrage- the right of citizens to vote in an election.

Theocracy- a form of government where religion and politics are not separated, and where the clergy play an important role in the political life of the country.

Totalitarian government- A government which controls all aspects of life in a country- the political, the social and the economic.

Topics for discussion:

1. Do you think that democracy can work in all countries of the world? Why?

2. In the 1990s many countries in Eastern Europe transitioned from a totalitarian form of government (communism) to democracy. What do you think are the greatest challenges in such a transition?

Questions:

1. How is democracy different from other forms of government?

    ____

    ____

    ____

    ____

    ____

2. Why do you think that separation of powers so important in a democracy?

    ____

    ____

    ____

    ____

    ____

3. Give some examples of individual rights mentioned in the constitution of your country.

    ____

    ____

    ____

4. Give an example of a theocracy. How is life like for the citizens of a theocracy?

5. What does « equality before the law » mean?

3.   Political Parties and Ideologies

Pluralism, a concept mentioned in the former two chapters, means that in a democratic system there is a diversity of political beliefs, values, and groups with different aims. Some groups have direct access to political power or influence while others have indirect access to political power by exerting pressure on politicians. These groups are called **interest groups**. Some examples of interest groups are human rights organizations, animal rights organizations, civil organizations, trade unions etc., which represent the views of their members. Although interest groups do not have direct access to political power because they do not participate in elections, they can exert pressure on politicians. Politicians can promise the representatives of pressure groups to favor their interests in exchange for votes.

3.1.   Political Parties

As previously stated in the first chapter, **political parties** are the entities in a democracy which directly participate in elections by naming candidates who run for office in elections. Political parties are represented in Parliament or Congress, and their delegates draft and vote on law initiatives. In most democracies, an organization must have a minimum number of members in order to become a political party.

In a democratic political system, there must be <u>at least two political parties</u> that citizens can choose from. One-party systems are not democratic because citizens have no choice. In other words, for a political party to exist in a democracy, there must be at least a competing political party. This fact is often forgotten or ignored when politicians as well as citizens use blackmailing, intimidation, violence, or other undemocratic methods to silence their opponents.

Political parties campaigning in Sweden before the 2018 elections. Sweden is a multiparty parliamentary democracy.

Political parties have many functions: from recruitment of candidates, debating and campaigning to governing, if they are the victors of the election. Political parties must look for candidates who represent their **party program** or **ideology** and are charismatic, so that they win the votes of the people. Presenting different points of view and debating them is also a typical function of a political party. Potential voters have many interests which might clash, for example the interests of employers and those of workers. Thus, political parties must give priority to certain interests over others. Furthermore, the dynamic nature of modern societies requires a constant revision of principles, values, and issues stated in the party program.

When a political election is coming, political parties help their candidates campaign for office. Campaigning is quite expensive, and therefore political parties must obtain donations from members and sympathizers.

Finally, if a political party (or a group of parties in a multiparty democracy) win an election, they get to run the government. Running the government means transforming the party's principles into law initiatives and thence to new laws. In a multiparty democracy, parties might form a **coalition** and compromise with other political parties so they can run the government together.

Citizens can support the political party they sympathize with as volunteers during campaigns. Examples of volunteering include distributing fliers, representing the party at the booths, sending letters to citizens, organizing events, and contributing economically. Citizens can become members of a political party and vote in the party's internal elections to designate candidates. Party members can also be postulated as candidates and run for office.

Another important function of political parties in the 21st century is establishing relations with parties in other countries which share their ideology or values. This is especially important in the European Union, where parties are represented at the international level at the European Parliament.

3.1.1.   What is a Party Program?

A party program is the set of principles, goals and **ideology** that describe the nature of a political party. The party program is in other words what the party stands for. While it is not expected that party members and voters totally agree with all the points of the program of a political party, it is important to read the program of a party before voting.

The party program describes the position of the political party regarding different issues like human rights, economic policy, labor policy, environmental policy, international trade, and foreign policy. While party programs are not written on stone and are modified according to the current economic, political, and international situation, they tend to be stable. They provide the voters with the information they need to know about the party so they can choose the right party to vote for.

3.1.2. Democratic and Undemocratic political parties

As stated in the first chapter, democracy means government by the people. It means that the people elect their representatives through elections every given period. And it means that the elected officials are **public servants** whose duty is to represent the interests of the people who voted them into office, and to step down if they lose an election to another party, or in some cases, if the people demand that they leave due to corruption or incompetence.

<u>Political parties that see democracy as an end, and not only as an instrument to attain political power are democratic parties.</u> In contrast, there are political parties that have authoritarian or totalitarian ideologies, and whose aim is to attain power but not to give it up once they run the government. These parties are not democratic. An example of an undemocratic party which came to power using democratic means but once in power destroyed democracy is the National Socialist Party (Nazi) party of Germany, which held power between 1933 and 1945.

Parties which do not recognize the equality of all citizens before the law are not democratic either. While, as has been stated before, there are differences between citizens and non-citizens of a state, in a democracy every citizen (born or naturalized) has the right to vote and is entitled to the same treatment as all other citizens, independently of her personal characteristics. This right can only be taken away from an individual in special circumstances, like if the person has committed a crime and is serving time in prison or is mentally ill.

An activist of the NPD (National Democratic Party) demonstrating in Germany. The NPD has been classified by the German Supreme Court as antidemocratic since it is against the equality of all citizens before the law, limits citizenship to ethnicity, and views democracy exclusively as a means to obtain power. However, the party has not been forbidden as of 2021.

In non-democracies, usually there is only one political organization that can run the country. Sometimes it may be called "political party", but there is no political competition; citizens have no choice. An example of a one-party system is the People's Republic of China. The only existing party is the Chinese Communist Party. All opposition to it is illegal, and dissidents are considered criminals and treated as such.

While the Nazi party in Germany came to power through free elections, the Communist Party obtained power in China through force, namely, after an armed revolt. As will be seen below, communist parties see democracy only as a means to attain power with the aim of creating a "dictatorship of the proletariat". Thus, communism does not provide a mechanism for the peaceful transfer of power.

3.2.   Political Ideologies

3.2.1.   What is an ideology?

As its name implies, an **ideology** is a set of ideas, of values and a vision of the world. An ideology is therefore not based on facts, but on opinions. In the case of religious ideologies, they are also based on superstition and dogma, and have been declared "sacred"- for this reason, they may not be questioned. Ideologies can be extremely dangerous because as "ready packages of thought", individuals are not encouraged to use their own judgement. Individuals who blindly follow what leaders say do not question whether the values, opinions, and principles expressed by the leaders are based on facts. Time and again history has shown that individuals who blindly follow an ideology can kill people for simply not agreeing with their view of the world.

Ideological education is called **indoctrination.** Indoctrination is used in authoritarian and totalitarian regimes to instrumentalize the citizens so that these do not question the ideology of their leaders, be them political or religious. Indoctrination is part of the school curricula in authoritarian, totalitarian, and theocratic governments, where the state controls the lives of its subjects. Indoctrination takes away from individuals their capacity to think for themselves and reach their own conclusions. The aim of indoctrination is to create uniformity of thought, so that the citizenry can be better controlled by the state. Although indoctrination is typical of authoritarian, totalitarian, and theocratic regimes, it is also present in democratic regimes but to a lesser degree.

The difference is that in democratic systems there is not one ideology, like is the case of authoritarian, totalitarian, or theocratic governments, but rather a plurality of ideologies. This plurality of ideologies reflects the pluralism of political parties. Ideally, in a democracy the citizen can choose from a set of ideologies the one or the ones that are best, or that best match with the individual's personal values.

Furthermore, in a democratic system which reflects ideological pluralism undemocratic ideologies are not forbidden, like it happens in authoritarian, totalitarian or theocratic governments. Although some ideologies are totally opposed to democratic values, <u>governments do not usually forbid them in democratic systems because forbidding an ideology or ideologies goes against the core of the democratic system, which is pluralism.</u> However, while ideologies which endorse violence might be tolerated, the use of violence is punishable by law. In a multiparty democracy many different ideologies are represented. Some of them will be described in this course.

3.2.2. Conservatism

As its name implies, the aim of conservatism is to <u>conserve what exists</u>. If change is needed, it should be examined and approached cautiously, because change can result in creating greater evils than the ones that it was intended to remedy. Conservatives cherish individualism and liberty. However, they see the need for a power to restrain the interests of individuals in the name of common good. Furthermore, conservatism is non-egalitarian: the followers of this ideology believe that, since some individuals contribute to society more than others, privilege is justified. However, like in all other democratic ideologies, conservatives believe in the equality of all citizens before the law. Conservatism favors a "small" government- this means that the individual should not be dependent on the state for his or her economic security, and that the state should interfere as little as possible in the economy. For conservatives, the role of the state is primarily to guarantee law and order.

3.2.3. Liberalism

The main difference between conservatism and liberalism is their view on equality. While conservatives believe that some people contribute to society more than others and are therefore entitled to privilege, liberals are much more **egalitarian**. For liberals, the state has the obligation to intervene in the economy and the society to create more equality. In other words, governments should be more involved in defending human rights. This includes measures to combat poverty, inequality, homelessness, discrimination, and other injustices. For liberals, people cannot become truly free until they are liberated from obstacles like the ones mentioned above. However, liberals think that the state should only intervene to foster, but never to limit freedom. This in practice can be quite difficult.

Liberals are much more accepting of issues like abortion and same-sex marriage than conservatives since they consider them issues of personal choice. Liberals favor more government intervention to help the needy and to protect individual liberties.

3.2.4. Social democracy

Social democracy developed as an ideology in Europe within trade unions, with the aim of defending the interests of the working class. Social democratic parties created the welfare state in many European countries like Germany, the Netherlands, and the Scandinavian countries. For social democrats, the worth of the individual is independent from his or her economic performance. The main ideal of social democratic parties is to create both the material and the legal conditions to ensure the freedom and the equality of all citizens and to foster their equal participation in education, labor, social security, culture, and democracy. Social democrats are against the unequal distribution of wealth, and therefore favor higher taxes for those who earn more. They see income differences as a hindrance to social development. Social democracy is envisioned as a society of free and equal individuals that needs an economic, social and state structure that can guarantee civil, political, social and economic rights for everyone. For social democrats, the principle of solidarity is of great importance.

3.2.5. Communism (or Marxism)

Communism is an ideology created by Karl Marx and Friedrich Engels in the 19th century. For Marx and Engels, <u>the ownership of the means of</u>

production (that is, factories, farms, shops, etc.) is what determines relations between people. Marx and Engels divide humanity into basically two groups: capitalists and **proletarians**. Capitalists are the owners of the means of production and exploit proletarians, who are the workers.

For communists, this exploitation of man by man is the source of all injustice and suffering in society, and the only way of achieving peace and harmony is to abolish private property by means of a revolution. They thought that after the proletarian revolution eliminated capitalism and private property, a dictatorship of the proletariat would be established, which would later lead to a communist society, a society of "perfect equality".

In practice, though, this never happened. While some countries did have a revolution instigated by communist agitators, the only thing that happened is that the means of production just changed owners- from capitalists to government bureaucrats. Furthermore, since planned economies were established, competition was practically non-existent and economic progress very modest in communist planned economies. Communism ceased to exist in Eastern Europe in the 1990s after the Berlin Wall was torn and the "iron curtain" fell. Former communist countries went back to capitalist (market) economies.

One of the worst characteristics of communism, as a one-party system, was intolerance. Dissidents, or people who disagreed with the government, were often fired from their jobs, arrested, and incarcerated merely for having opinions which differed from the views of the government. Millions of people in many countries of the world lost their lives as a result of the imposition of communism. Communism is thus an undemocratic ideology.

3.2.6. Fascism

Fascism is a doctrine created by the Italian dictator Benito Mussolini. Fascism is an anti-democratic ideology because it allows no organizations outside of the state. Fascism stresses the importance of the state above all other organizations: Only through the state can the individual find her true essence. Furthermore, fascism does not accept the equality of all individuals before the law. Fascism sees in suffrage and democracy nothing but delusion. As Mussolini himself put it: democratic regimes make people believe that they can exercise sovereignty through suffrage, but in reality, sovereignty is exercised by "irresponsible and secret forces". Fascism sees the state not only as a territorial, military, or economic entity, but also as a spiritual and ethical conception.

As a non-democratic ideology, there is no formula in fascism for the peaceful transfer of power from one leader to his successor. Moreover, fascism stresses the right of strong states to conquer other, weaker states, and views states which exercise their sovereignty within their borders without expansionist aims as "decadent".

While fascism as an active political force was vanquished after World War II, fascist parties still exist in many countries.

3.2.7. Feminism

Although vastly different people who belong to quite different social classes and have totally different aspirations call themselves "feminists", one characteristic that all of these people have in common is that they believe that women are -at least- equal to men and that they have been systematically discriminated and oppressed by them, and by a superstructure created by men that they define as the "patriarchy".

Many feminists believe in **social constructionism**, a political view that states that all roles and identities, including gender, are "social constructions". They see that while biological sex is determined by nature, gender roles are acquired. For the more radical feminists, the oppression of women by men precedes all other forms of oppression. Therefore, one of their aims is to get rid of gendered social roles, like typical family roles, and of masculinity.

3.2.8. Nationalism

Nationalists see the nation as a group of people united by ethnicity, language, history, traditions, and values. Nationalists are opposed to mass immigration and multiculturalism because they see in them a threat to destabilize the nation-state by forcing together people who share neither ethnicity, nor language, history, traditions, or values.

For nationalists, the interests of the nation-state have precedence over global interests. They see the power granted by governments to supranational organizations like the European Union, the United Nations, and the World Bank as a threat to the sovereignty of the state. While nationalists are not opposed to international trade and cooperation, for them the interests of the nation have priority over global interests.

Furthermore, nationalists see most other political parties as globalist, that is, that they favor global financial and economic interests over the interests of their own people and their own nation. Nationalists, in contrast, favor state control of strategic industries and resources, with the aim of preventing the state from being disempowered by strong multinational corporations and supranational organizations.

President Andrzej Duda, from the Polish nationalist party Law and Justice, during the summer 2020 political campaign.

Glossary

Coalition- In a multiparty system, when two or more parties decide to govern together.

Egalitarian- Favoring equality among individuals.

Indoctrination- Inculcation of tenets or principles with the aim of deterring the individual from using his or her own judgement.

Interest groups- Organizations that aim to peacefully influence the decisions taken by politicians, so that these favor the group's interests.

Party program- The ideals, goals, tenets and aims of a party expressed in a program. The program is usually divided in different topics, like labor policy, economic policy, foreign policy, etc.

Proletarian- In Marxist ideology, worker who is exploited by the capitalist, and who rebels in a revolution.

Public servant- Any person who works for the public administration. S/he may or may not be affiliated to a political party.

Social constructionism- A theory that states that our understanding of the world is based on shared assumptions. For social constructionists, gender is not determined by genes, but a socially constructed concept.

Topics for discussion

1. Should a democratic government forbid undemocratic parties and organizations? Why?

2. Do you think it is important for citizens to read the programs of all political parties before they vote?

Questions

1. Give two examples of interest groups. What or whose interests do they defend?

____

____

____

____

____

2. Name at least three functions of political parties.

____

____

____

____

3. What is the main difference between 'democratic' and 'undemocratic' political parties?

____

____

____

____

4. Why can ideologies become dangerous? Give an example.

____

____

____

____

____

5. Are communist parties democratic? Why or why not?

____

____

____

____

____

6. Is there a 'democratic' ideology? Why?

____

____

____

____

____

4.   The Democratic Society

Democracy does not only imply a political system, but also a way of living. Democracy is based upon pluralism. **Tolerance,** which can best be defined as the peaceful coexistence of differences, is a precondition of pluralism. Tolerance does not mean that we must like the beliefs, the lifestyles, or the behavior of others. <u>However, it does mean that we must respect them</u>, as long as others respect us and respect the law. Furthermore, the principle of **equality before the law** means that laws apply to everyone: there are no special laws for special groups, as is the case in theocratic or other non-democratic states.

4.1.   Civil society and politics

In totalitarian states, like for example Cuba or North Korea, the state controls every aspect of the citizens' lives. All clubs, associations, leagues, and organizations are either directly run by the state or strictly controlled by it. In Cuba, for example, all children are obliged to belong to a circle of "young pioneers" which in reality are nothing but indoctrination institutes where they are instructed what to think, how to think, and to denounce anybody, including their parents, if they express opinions critical of the government.

The presence of NGOs is either non-existent or limited in totalitarian systems because NGOs cannot be controlled by the state and are often critical of the actions of governments against their citizens. Freedom of religion is likewise curtailed in totalitarian societies: In communist countries, some, if not all religions are forbidden.

In theocracies, there is one "official" religion, which means that it is illegal to have beliefs that differ from that religion. People are forced to practice the state religion, independently of whether they believe in its tenets or not and can be harshly punished for not following the rites and traditions prescribed by that religion. In Saudi Arabia, for example, the "religious police" has the authority of arresting women for not being "properly dressed", or for being in the company of men who are not their relatives, since this conduct goes against the official religion. In Iran, declaring that God does not exist is punishable by death.

In contrast, the division between the civil and the political society is one of the main pillars of democracy: In Western democracies, citizens may join any group or organization as long as it respects the rule of law. Citizens may leave a religious organization for any reason, and they need not provide explanations to anyone. Likewise, citizens can convert to the religion of their choice or not practice a religion at all.

In democracies there is a plurality of civic organizations that represent citizens' interests. These organizations are usually financed by private donors, enterprises, or other organizations. Examples of these are children's rights organizations, women's rights organizations, animal rights organizations, authors' organizations, and journalists' organizations.

China is an example of a highly authoritarian regime with a one-party system. Religious freedom as well as freedom of speech, freedom of the press and the right to demonstrate are practically non-existent in that communist state. Criticism of the regime is harshly punished. However, China has a market economy.

https://democracyandeducation.org

4.2. The strict division between private life and public life

While citizens' lives are strictly controlled in authoritarian, totalitarian and theocratic societies, in democratic societies the citizen chooses the lifestyle that best suits her. Citizens of democratic societies can choose their profession, how to dress, who to date or marry, what music to listen to, etc. In other words, citizens choose how to live their lives.

In theocratic societies it is the family who decides who a person (usually a woman) will marry. In Saudi Arabia, for example, marriages are arranged, as in many so-called honor-societies. Furthermore, different rules apply to men and to women: While men are entitled to four wives and can divorce at will, women must obey the wishes of her family and after marriage the wishes of her husband. A woman who does not obey may be harshly chastised. Having sex before marriage for women is an offence that can be punishable by death.

Another example is same-sex marriage. While same-sex marriage is not legally recognized in many countries which have a democratic political system, homosexuality is not criminalized because having a romantic relationship or living with someone belongs to the private realm of the individual's life. While the parents of a gay man may disapprove of his union with another man, they may not punish him for his choice. This is not the case in many traditional authoritarian societies, where the relatives of a person assume that they "have the right" to kill him because he happens to like people of the same sex. "Honor killings" are illegal in democracies and carry long jail sentences. While a traditional, religious family may decide not to have contact with a homosexual son or a lesbian daughter, they have no right whatsoever to interfere in the lives of their children.

While it is true that same-sex marriage is frowned upon in many democratic countries, only in democracies is it possible for non-heterosexual people to defend their rights by joining civic or other human rights organizations. Likewise, in many democratic countries it is illegal to discriminate against a person for her sexual orientation. An employer who discriminates against a non-heterosexual employee can face a lawsuit that can cost a lot of money.

Two women getting married in Guadalajara, Mexico in 2019. Same-sex marriage is now accepted in most states of Mexico.

4.3.   The Secular Society

What is a secular society? It is a society where the political and the religious spheres are separate and totally independent from each other. In a democratic, **secular** society there is no "official religion". That is, there is a plurality of religious organizations, just like a plurality of parties in the political realm, and religion is a choice. Religious leaders are subjected to the authority of the state and should not get involved in politics. Furthermore, preaching political content which jeopardizes the democratic order in religious sermons is an offence in many democracies.

In a secular society, following religious tenets is optional, but <u>obeying the law is mandatory.</u> In other words, if the tenets of a religion conflict with the law of a country, <u>the law of the country must be followed.</u>

As has been mentioned, democracy is based on the principle of the equality of all citizens before the law. This is not the case in certain religions, where women are subordinated to men, and where members of different religions are not granted equality. Therefore, if the religion of a citizen conflicts with the laws of the state, the citizen must follow the law or face criminal charges.

A family father, for example, may not force his daughter to marry someone she does not like, nor forbid her from having contact with men. The father and the daughter have equal rights in a democracy. While parents must assume responsibility for their children and respect the law, they may not make choices that violate the rights of the children. <u>In democracies children have rights too.</u> And parents who do not respect the rights of their children violate the law.

In civilized, Western democracies animals are entitled to protection as well. Therefore, if an individual follows a religious principle calling for unnecessary animal cruelty (like ritual slaughter, forbidden in many countries), and animal cruelty is punishable by law, the individual can face criminal charges and be convicted.

What does "freedom of religion" mean in a democracy?

Freedom of religion means that a person cannot be discriminated against or prosecuted because of her religious beliefs. However, <u>these beliefs are strictly individual.</u> This implies that parents cannot force their children to follow the tenets of a religion if the children do not want to. Nor does it mean that a religious leader has the right to kill somebody in the name of religion because that individual has decided to leave. Neither does freedom of religion imply that some citizens are exempt from fulfilling their obligations in the name of religion, or that their children are exempt from going to school or participating in the school's activities because these conflict with the tenets of their religion.

Freedom of religion guarantees that people of different religions have the same rights. <u>It never grants special rights to a group of citizens.</u> As stated above, in a democracy the law is above all religions.

Freedom of religion does not grant religious individuals the right to punish people who, in their view, have offended their religious views. While all people are free to criticize what they dislike, they cannot take justice in their own hands. <u>Freedom of religion includes the right to leave a religion or to criticize it without facing consequences.</u>

4.4.   The Rule of Law

While citizens are entitled to certain individual rights in a democracy, like freedom of speech, freedom of the press, freedom to demonstrate peacefully, religious freedom, etc., a democratic order does not mean that a person can do as she wishes and disregard the law.

In a democracy, <u>only the police have the right to use violence</u> when a situation so requires. While in some democratic countries citizens who have fulfilled certain requisites can possess firearms (for self-defense, for example), only the authorities can impart justice. If a citizen feels that she has been wronged by another citizen or by the state, there is a <u>legal process that must be followed</u> to redress a wrong committed against her.

Obeying the police is not a choice; it is mandatory, because the police are the representatives of the law in a state. While a citizen can file a lawsuit against a police officer if the officer uses unnecessary force, for example, the citizen cannot decide whether she wants to follow the orders of the officer.

<u>In case of an emergency the state has the authority to limit or suppress civil rights.</u> An example of this is when a state imposes a curfew after violent riots in a city. While citizens usually have freedom of movement,

this freedom can be restricted under special circumstances, and the people who do not respect these restrictions can be prosecuted. Another example is for public health reasons, where gatherings can be either limited to a certain number of people or forbidden during a certain period.

Glossary

Equality before the law- The laws of a country apply equally to all citizens independently of their gender, their age, their wealth, or any other individual attribute.

Freedom of religion- The right of citizens to profess the religion of their choice, to convert to any religion or to leave a religion without facing consequences.

Rule of law- The mandatory nature of the laws and regulations, which must be followed by all citizens independently of whether they agree with them or not.

Secular state- A state in which the realms of politics and religion are completely separate.

Tolerance- the peaceful coexistence of differences.

Topics for discussion

1. Do you think that religious leaders have the right of publicly expressing their political opinions in a democracy? Why?

2. Do you think that in a democracy citizens should have the right to bear arms? Why?

Questions

1. Give an example of tolerance.

____

____

____

____

____

2. In your opinion, when should the state take children away from their parents?

____

____

____

____

____

3. Do you think that an employer in a democracy has the right to demand a certain dress code from his or her employees? Why?

____

____

____

____

4. Do you feel free to leave your religion (if you have one) and convert to another religion without facing reprisals? Why?

____

____

____

____

____

5. How would you react if a police officer unjustly arrested you, or if he used unnecessary force?

____

____

____

____

____

5. Democratic Political Culture

5.1. Definition of Political Culture

Political culture can best be defined as all the attitudes and values that a people or a nation have about government and politics. Political culture is the product of the history, the traditions, the institutions, the values, and the culture of a nation. For this reason, political culture is different from country to country, even if the countries considered are all democracies. However, there are certain characteristics common to the political culture of all democratic countries, like **pluralism, tolerance,** and the **equality of all citizens before the law.**

Political culture affects the way individuals behave, how they respond to laws and how they formulate their demands to their leaders: While in countries with a high degree of political institutionalization leaders are considered legitimate, people tend to respect the laws and regulations, in countries where politicians are considered corrupt and where democracy is young (for example, after a transition from an authoritarian system), people tend to circumvent or disregard laws.

5.2. Agents of political culture

School

The acquisition of political culture begins during childhood, in our homes and at school. The textbooks that children use in school are determinant in shaping political culture. The state uses textbooks to educate pupils the way they want their future citizens to be. Very often, textbooks are a source of **indoctrination** more than a source of information.

The educational boards of countries and states are the ones who determine the content of textbooks: the symbols, the values, the attitudes that are praised and the ones that are discouraged or criticized determine which behavior the state expects of its future citizens.

Ideally, textbooks in a democracy reflect the pluralism of the political system. However, different administrations or governments in a same state can have differing values.

Teachers play a crucial role in the shaping of political culture. While teachers in the primary and secondary school are compelled to follow strict curricula imposed by the state, the situation is different at the tertiary level. In democracies, higher education must tolerate **academic freedom,** which means that professors who have different political views can present them to their students without being censured or afraid of consequences. An example of academic freedom is the books that the teaching staff at the tertiary level use for their courses: the books might be about the same topic, but with totally different perspectives. However, some intolerant views are forbidden even in democracies, and professors who present them can be terminated and prosecuted.

The Media

Another important agent of political culture is the **media**. Radio stations, TV channels, newspapers and magazines play a pivotal role in the politization of the people. In democracies the media reflects the pluralism of the political system. This means that different newspapers will present events from different perspectives. A fundamental component of democratic political culture is **transparency.** Transparency means that journalists are free to publish any true story about anybody or any organization as long as they respect a code of ethics. In democracies, journalists do not "disappear", nor are they poisoned, murdered, or incarcerated for their publications.

However, the fact that a democracy is based on pluralism does not mean that the media is free from **censorship.** Again, the government decides which content is published and which content is censored, and these decisions do not necessarily depend on whether the content is true or not. Moreover, in many countries the government decides which newspapers and magazines obtain funding. Typically, publications which are friendly to the government obtain more funding than those which are critical of it.

A problem with **freedom of the press** is that to exercise that freedom you must first own a magazine or newspaper. Ordinary citizens do not usually own mass media, and for this reason their views are neglected or ignored in favor of the views of the government, or of the organizations who support the government.

Social Media

Nowadays, the role of social media in politics has become incredibly influential, even competing with the mass media. The fact that any citizen can post on social media like Facebook, Twitter or Instagram means that the mass media has lost its monopoly on information and that the state can no longer act as censor. While the advent of social media has meant that the political arena has opened up to new actors who formerly did not have a means to express opinions and views, it also carries great dangers, like spreading disinformation, fake news, slander and rumors. Many social movements, protests and demonstrations have been started using the social media. Politicians use social media to communicate with citizens, and during political campaigns social media are an important tool used by candidates and political parties to win voters. However, the responsible use of social media means that the citizen must first check facts before arriving at conclusions, and not believe everything that is posted just because it has been posted.

Books

Ideally, in democracies all books representing all different perspectives are available for the citizens. While this might be the case even in young democracies in the developing world, books are of little or no use if the population has a low educational level or is illiterate.

Again, authors who want to exercise their freedom of the press must first have their books approved by a publishing company; otherwise, it can be expensive for an author to self-publish a book. Publishing companies are not usually owned by ordinary citizens but by corporate organizations which have their own interests.

Cultured and educated people are much more difficult to manipulate than uneducated or illiterate people, because educated people know their rights and can demand redress from their government if their rights are not respected. Therefore, some governments are not keen on investing on education and critical thinking, since this would mean relinquishing power over to the people they govern.

5.3.   The forging of national identity

National identity is the group we identify with, its values, its norms and customs, and our pride in our nationality. While our **nationality** reflects our culture, mores and customs, it not always coincides with our **citizenship. Citizenship** means that a person owes allegiance to a certain state and is entitled to all the rights granted by that state. Citizenship can be by birth or by **naturalization**, that is, obtained through a legal process.

An individual may be born in a certain country, but maybe his parents come from another country. He can decide which citizenship to take when he comes of age (usually at 18). Likewise, many people who move to another country for any reason and stay for a minimum number of years can become citizens by **naturalization** if they fulfil certain requisites.

National identity is not as important in some countries as it is in others: While some governments pursue a strong national identity (nationalists, for example) for others national identity plays a much less important role.

Forging national identity in pupils: Mexican children saluting their flag. (Image courtesy of the municipality of San Martín de Hidalgo, Jalisco, Mexico)

5.4.   The characteristics of democratic political culture

While democracies can vary enormously depending on the history, the values and the traditions of each country, democratic political culture has certain basic elements that distinguish it from the political culture of authoritarian, totalitarian, or theocratic states.

The Rule of Law

It can be quite difficult for people who come from non-democratic regimes to understand the principle of the division of powers. People who come from authoritarian, nepotist regimes, where the executive controls the justice system, often cannot understand that in a democracy the head of state or head of government does not have power over the courts, and that even representatives of the law, like policemen, are accountable for their actions.

Secularism

People who have grown up in theocracies and who are used to obeying the dictates of religious leaders are often disconcerted when they come to a democratic country, with a strict separation between the political and the religious realms. As has been stated before, in a democracy religion is a choice, not an obligation. Furthermore, if there is a clash between religious values and the laws of the state the second have supremacy over the first.

An example of a clash of religious values and state laws is freedom of speech: While some religions consider the questioning of their tenets a "sin" which deserves punishment, in a democracy people can exercise their freedom of speech by harshly criticizing a religion. Religious leaders who feel offended may not punish the "sinners" in any way in a democracy, except for banning them from their temples.

Equality of all citizens before the law

In some countries, some individuals are entitled to more rights than others: In countries like Afghanistan and Saudi Arabia, women are subjected to the authority of male relatives. Women cannot take decisions on their own and cannot live their lives according to their own wishes.

In Saudi Arabia, the guardianship system guarantees that women are subjected to the authority of men for absolutely everything—from getting an education, to getting married or divorced. Women in Saudi Arabia are under the authority of male relatives in the same way that small children are under the custody of the parents in Western countries. In Saudi Arabia there are specific laws for men and for women. Another example is India: Formerly, the caste system gave different rights and privileges to people of different castes, or social classes.

In Afghanistan, there are laws for men and laws for women. Women must bear a burqa when they leave their home or face harsh punishments.

<u>In a democracy the same laws apply to everyone, independently of their sex, social status, age, wealth, religion, or any other characteristic.</u> While parents have custody over their underage children in democracies, child protective services might decide to take the child from the family if the parents do not respect the rights of the child. In a democracy there is no other law than the law of the state within the state jurisdiction, that is, within its boundaries. Citizens who do not respect the rights of other citizens in the name of culture or tradition are prosecuted.

Tolerance

As has been previously discussed, <u>tolerance implies the peaceful coexistence of differences.</u> In a democracy, even if we dislike the lifestyle of some people because it totally differs from ours, we are obliged to respect them: If, for example, a young man decides to abandon his religion and follow his own convictions, the parents have nothing to say; or if a young woman discovers that she is a lesbian and decides to have a partner of the same sex, this is considered a personal choice. Attacking people for their personal choices is illegal and punishable in a democracy. Furthermore, freedom of speech means not only that we have a right to express our own opinions, but that <u>others whose opinions we dislike or strongly disagree with also have the right of expressing theirs.</u>

Pluralism

As has been stated before, there can be no democracy without pluralism. Firstly, pluralism implies that there is a distinction between the state and its institutions and government, which is the party or parties which exercise political power during a certain period. Pluralism does not exist in authoritarian systems, where the distinction between state and government is blurred or non-existent. However, pluralism does not only refer to the existence of more than one political party, but also to the existence of multiple religious associations, interest groups, cultural groups and independent groups that are not controlled by the state.

Strict separation of the private and the public life realms

In a democracy we sometimes have to deal with people who lead a life we don't agree with: Traditional, religious people sometimes have gay people as colleagues; liberal people sometimes have to take the services provided by nationalists, and students have to tolerate other students who might have totally opposing political views.

This is only possible in a democracy, where the private and the public realms of life are strictly separated. As has been stated above, in a democracy religion is a choice, as is having a sex life or not having it. The way a person leads her private life does not play a role in the public life of the individual. Moreover, not respecting the private life of people is against the law in democracies, like for example denying a job to somebody based on their religious beliefs or their sexual orientation.

Citizens have a right to dress the way they want to (albeit not the right to go around naked!). Exceptions to this right are the dress codes that some employers have for their staff during working hours. This is definitely not the case in theocracies like Iran or Saudi Arabia, where women can be harshly punished for not wearing a headscarf or for showing their arms or their legs. Not respecting the right of others to lead the lives they want is punishable by law in a democracy.

5.5. Democratic political culture and democratic behavior

An individual who has grown up in a democratic political culture views equality before the law, tolerance, pluralism, the rule of law and the separation of the public and the private realms as normal elements of the society. However, it is difficult for immigrants from authoritarian, totalitarian, or theocratic systems to understand and accept all the elements of a democratic political culture. Furthermore, even people who grew up in democracies sometimes forget that the citizen has rights and duties as well, and that the same laws apply to everyone.

The 21st century has witnessed a political polarization in many democratic countries. Certain members of political parties seem to forget that their political opponents have the same freedom of speech and freedom to demonstrate peacefully as they do.

Peaceful demonstration for the rights of animals in London, United Kingdom in 2016.

Counterdemonstrations, <u>which are a disregard to the right of others to demonstrate</u>, have become commonplace, many times ending in violent clashes.

Violent attacks against non-heterosexual people with no other reason than their sexual orientation have become more common, with the mass immigration of people from cultures where homosexuality is considered criminal. Likewise, religious leaders who have immigrated to democracies from non-democratic countries seem to ignore the secular nature of the state they have voluntarily chosen as their home.

Democratic behavior means practicing the principles of democratic political culture in our daily lives, even if that implies tolerating people, ideas or organizations we strongly disagree with.

Glossary

Academic freedom – Freedom that the teaching staff at the tertiary level have from the control of the state or other controls on their academic activities, like teaching and doing research.

Censorship – Government control of mass media; of deciding which information will be published and which will not.

Citizenship – Legal bond between an individual and a state. Citizenship can be the product of nationality or of naturalization.

Freedom of the press – Freedom to express our opinions in written form.

Mass media – Television, radio, newspapers, and other sources of information.

Nationality – The bond an individual has to a nation. The nationality of an individual is determined by the nationality of the parents or the place of birth.

Naturalization – Obtaining citizenship in a country other than an individual's country of origin through a legal process.

Political culture – The attitudes, values, and views that an individual or a group of individuals have about politics.

Transparency – The right of the citizens to accurate information.

Topics for discussion

1. Democracies grant freedom of religion to the citizens. What do you think should be the limits to religious freedom in a democracy?

2. Should an individual who applies for naturalization in a democratic country first pass a basic test on the tenets of democracy? Why?

Questions

1. What are the characteristics of the political culture of your country of origin?

____

____

____

____

____

2. Give two examples of how school shapes the political culture of the pupils.

____

____

____

____

____

3. Do you think that the state should have the right to censor information, even if it is true?

____

____

____

____

____

4. What is the difference between nationality and citizenship?

____

____

____

____

____

5. What does "equality of all citizens before the law" mean?

____

____

____

____

____

6. What duties does a citizen have in a democracy?

____

____

____

____

7. In a democratic political culture, how does a citizen react when she hears opinions she strongly dislikes?

____

____

____

____

____

8. One of the civic rights of democratic systems is the right to demonstrate. What limits should there be to the right to demonstrate?

____

____

____

____

____

6.   The Enemies of Democracy

While democracy gives the citizen more rights than she can possibly have than in any other political system, democracy is a fragile form of government that is constantly threatened by forces which oppose its basic tenets. Furthermore, democracy must constantly renew itself when new needs or new demands of the citizens arise.

We saw in chapter 5 that there are democratic and undemocratic ideologies and parties, that is, <u>ideologies and parties which see democracy only as a means to attain power, and, once in power, destroy the democratic order.</u> While there are many significant differences among political parties and ideologies, the most crucial difference is whether political parties view democracy as an end in itself or only as a means to obtain power. This is the cornerstone of democracy: it is the people who, through suffrage, every given interval of time get to elect their representatives and rulers.

As we have seen before, representatives and decision-makers are also called **public servants**, because in a democracy their duty is precisely to serve their electors. However, very often politicians forget that they are public servants, and instead of serving their electors they aim to be served by them.

The aim of this chapter is to present and analyze some of the major enemies of democracy, which sometimes are overt and sometimes are covert. As has been discussed, the National Socialist (Nazi) party of Germany was elected to parliament by the people. However, once in power, the Nazi party forbade all other parties and dismantled any possible opposition. Civil rights were immediately abolished and expressing any opinion critical of the government became a crime. The Nazi party was obliterated in Germany with the end of World War II and forbidden in some countries. Nonetheless, nowadays there are national socialist parties and parties which sympathize with this ideology in some countries.

Likewise, Marxist (or communist) parties participate in elections in many democratic countries. While some of these parties might have modified their programs to fit democratic rules, the essence of Marxism is the overthrow of democracy with the aim of creating a dictatorship of the proletariat, as well as to ban private property. Marxism provides no formula for the peaceful transfer of power nor does it explain how political leaders will ever step down from power.

Democracy has other enemies, though, that are not so easily identifiable but that pose a threat to the rule of the people and to the exercise of civil rights. No democracy is perfect because human nature is far from perfect; However, only democracy can create a political culture of tolerance, pluralism, and transparency. Unfortunately, many citizens and rulers in democratic countries seem to forget or disregard these principles when respecting them is to their disadvantage.

6.1.   Demagoguery

The term demagoguery was used by the Greek philosopher Aristotle to designate an impure form of democracy, in which opportunistic politicians used their power to "serve themselves". **Demagogues** are individuals who say what their electors want to hear, but they seldom fulfill promises they give to the people. They distort the truth or lie to win adepts. It is very unfortunate that demagogues do not want their people to become educated, simply because educated people are much harder to deceive. Demagogues promise many things as candidates but once in power forget that they have a debt to the people who elected them to office. Therefore, demagoguery needs ignorance as a breeding ground.

6.2.   Ignorance

An educated people who knows how to distinguish facts from opinions, and who can think rationally is a threat to demagogues, because it will demand respect for its rights and hold its representatives accountable. A profoundly serious issue though is that it is precisely the state, and specifically the government in power, who decides what the curricular content of the education offered by the state will be.

Ignorance is not so much a state of not knowing as a state of not wanting to know, or of not wanting to question whatever information is provided by the state-censored media. The state favors ignorance when it censors critical content in radio broadcasts or TV shows, deciding for the citizens what is best for them. While it is unrealistic that citizens will always be informed about all current issues, the attitude of ignorance is that of not wanting to know, or of denial.

While there has never been a greater surplus of information than in the 21st century due to the ubiquitous use of the internet, disinformation, fake news, rumors, and slander abound, confusing citizens instead of informing them.

Disinformation can take the form of fake news, half-truths, and distorted data. Journalists, as businesspeople, want to sell their stories. Therefore, it is not the most accurate stories which sell best but rather the most sensational. It is an unfortunate fact that citizens do not usually do a fact-check of all the stories they read in social media, nor do they question what the source of the information they were given is.

While before the age of the internet there was a monopoly of information held by the mass media like radio stations, TV networks and newspapers, nowadays anyone can post anything on Facebook, Twitter, or Instagram. Very few people will fact-check to see whether the information they obtained is true, if it is distorted, or where the information comes from. Moreover, some people deceive others by creating photomontages and presenting them as true images in social media.

Ignorance is a threat to democracy because democracy is based on transparency. Lies, half-truths and fake news therefore undermine the right of the people to accurate information.

6.3.   Undemocratic behavior

The bases of a democratic political culture were presented in chapter 5. Undemocratic behavior are the attitudes that undermine the principles of the **rule of law**, **secularism**, the **equality of all citizens before the law**, **tolerance**, **pluralism**, and the strict **separation of private and public life.**

Demonstrations which turn into riots, where property is destroyed and people are hurt, attempt against the rule of law. Sometimes riots become so violent that the government is forced to issue a **curfew**, thereby curtailing the right of all citizens to free mobility.

A demonstration against police brutality that turned into a riot in Los Angeles, California, USA 2020.

Religious leaders who talk about politics in their sermons, or even incite their congregations to violence against the state and their institutions are a threat to democracy. Likewise, religious organizations that forbid the participation of their parishioners in politics undermine democracy.

While the right to demonstrate peacefully is granted to all citizens in a democracy, a counterdemonstration goes against the tenets of democracy because it curtails the right of another group of citizens to demonstrate. As stated before, we might strongly disagree with the views of other people and need not mingle with them; however, curtailing their right to demonstrate undermines democracy.

Likewise, putting labels on people disqualifies us for a serious debate, a real exchange of political ideas. <u>Labels and insults are not arguments</u>, and the only result of such attitudes is a greater distancing of people with different political opinions and polarization that can result in verbal or physical violence.

Many people, both those who grew up in democracies and immigrants from non-democratic countries, disregard the fact <u>that it is precisely pluralism what distinguishes a democratic system from an authoritarian system.</u> Conflict is natural and healthy, because it is a sign of the existence of differences of opinion. However, violence as a means to "solve" conflict is neither natural nor healthy.

6.4.   "Political Correctness" and self–censorship

In the polarized political climate of the 21st century, many people are afraid to say what they think, to express their opinions or to criticize policies that they consider wrong. While it can be quite unpleasant to have an altercation with an individual or a group who does not share our views, or who even has or have views which clash with ours, not defending our freedom of speech and our convictions enables undemocratic behavior and intolerance. While, as has been stated before, democracy does not give us the right to offend or threaten others, it does give us the right to stand for what we think.

Many people who dislike conflict are very often ignored or belittled for not defending their points of view. This happens often at the workplace with an undemocratic leadership, where some people think that they have the right to bully others because they do not agree with the majority. The same happens in schools, especially when teachers instead of fostering pluralism, indoctrinate their pupils. (See section 6.8 below).

When we see an injustice, no matter who commits it, and we remain quiet, we acknowledge it and enable the wrongdoer to continue committing injustices. Authoritarian leaders and despots base their authority on the silence of people who are afraid of expressing their criticism.

In democratic systems there are instances like for example trade unions or school boards where we can report unethical behavior, even if the individual who commits it happens to be our boss or our teacher.

6.5.   Corruption

Many people talk about the concept of "corruption" without exactly knowing what it means. "Corruption" is used to describe the embezzlement of public funds for private ends but has also other manifestations: As we have seen, democracy is based on the principle of **transparency,** that is, the right of the citizens to accurate information. Not providing accurate information to the citizenry is a form of corruption; or when some individual or group **bribes** a civil servant or a political party, we also talk about corruption. A person or organization who accepts a bribe will not act in the manner prescribed by law but will favor the interests of the person or the organization who paid the bribe.

Bribing is a profoundly serious phenomenon, because it undermines the principle of the equality of all citizens before the law. Only the most affluent or powerful members of the society can afford to bribe officials, therefore curtailing the rights of the poor and the disadvantaged, of the most vulnerable people.

Cronyism is a quite common form of corruption as well. This practice means that positions of importance are not given to the most skilled individuals but to friends and relatives. The result of this is that the most capable people will not be hired, but friends or relatives who in many cases lack the skills and the competencies necessary to fulfill the tasks of the position. While cronyism is a common practice in authoritarian or totalitarian systems where power is transferred from father to son or from sibling to sibling, in democracies it is the people who elect their officials. Cronyism exists at many levels: From party officers who offer positions to members of their families, to universities who hire the friends or lovers of professors, disregarding procedures that should guarantee that only the most qualified individuals obtain the vacant positions.

While **lobbyism** is not forbidden by law, this practice jeopardizes democracy. **Lobbies** are powerful organizations that offer <u>donations to political parties</u> in exchange for policies friendly to their interests. The main difference between a donation and a bribe is that the donation is made to a political party which uses it for campaigning, while a bribe goes to an officer's private bank account. The problem with lobbyism is that it fosters inequality: The most vulnerable members of society lack the economic means available to lobbies and can therefore not influence politicians as rich organizations can.

Examples of lobbies are the petroleum industry, the meat industry, and large corporations. The ones affected by the actions of lobbies cannot defend their interests because they are in a much weaker position. How can exploited workers, or families exposed to the toxic fumes of the petroleum industry compete with transnational companies? How can animals complain of the cruelty of factory farming, inhuman transport, and slaughter?

It is for this reason that only informed, responsible citizens can demand transparency from political parties and government officers. In a democracy it is the people who hold power and grant it to their representatives.

6.6.   Antidemocratic organizations

Antidemocratic organizations are those who oppose free elections, the equality of all citizens before the law as well as the rights granted to all citizens by the law. As we have seen before, there are democratic and antidemocratic parties, but there are also organizations other than political parties that pose a threat to democracy. Antidemocratic organizations usually employ violence and threats to intimidate or silence their opponents. They do not accept the principle of pluralism and harass politicians who do not kowtow to their demands. There are antidemocratic organizations with different political affiliations. However, while the ends they pursue might be totally contrary, the methods they employ to achieve those goals is what makes them similar.

The Ku Klux Klan is a white supremacist organization. They are against equal rights and the mingling of races. The members of this organization have been convicted many times of committing violent crimes against non-white people.

Terrorist organizations who claim to have the right to use violence to attain their goals are a threat to democracy. These organizations use tactics like intimidation, threats, and physical violence. They disregard the tenet of the rule of law and take justice in their own hands. These organizations can be of a religious nature, like Al Qaida, or of a political nature, like Antifa. In any case, while their ideologies differ, they have the use of violence and terror in common.

An Antifa demonstration against President Trump in 2017. Antifa organizations use violent methods to achieve their political goals.

Organized crime is similar in its tactics to terrorist organizations; however, their aims are different: Whereas terrorist organizations have a political agenda, the only aim of organized crime is to make money. Organized crime is involved in several unlawful activities like human trafficking, prostitution, money laundering, the illegal sale of drugs, the trade of human organs and of endangered animal and plant species.

Organized crime has become so vicious in some countries that the state authorities have ceased to function: In parts of Mexico, for example, drug cartels are so strong that they have systematically murdered government officials or forced them to resign.

Like terrorist organizations, organized crime does not respect the principle that the state has the monopoly of the use of violence. Organized crime threatens the democratic state by undermining its institutions and functions.

A young victim of human trafficking. Every year, hundreds of thousands of people are kidnapped and sold as slaves, prostitutes or to be used in organized crime. Criminals engaged in human trafficking have no scruples whatsoever.

6.7.   Political Indifference

A very great problem of democratic systems is low participation. While all citizens (except the ones purging a sentence in jail, the mentally retarded or others who for extraordinary circumstances may not vote) have a right to vote, a considerable percentage of them do not express their political will through suffrage.

In most of the cases, it is the people who would most benefit from change that do not vote, because they believe that their vote does not make a difference. Other people are so busy making ends meet that they simply lack the interest to vote. Still others have no faith in politicians whatsoever and see registering and voting as a waste of time. Moreover, political indifference strengthens the existing political structure and makes change even more unlikely. Politicians who face scrutiny are much more likely to fulfill their duties than those who feel that nobody controls their actions.

6.8. Teachers who indoctrinate

The mission of a teacher is to instruct students, to foster their critical thinking skills and prepare them to be responsible citizens. In a democracy, teachers must therefore teach students the importance of pluralism and tolerance, as well as practice these crucial democratic tenets in class. While teachers as citizens have a right to their own political opinions and preferences, they must recognize and respect the right their students have to their own political preferences and opinions.

Yet teachers forget their mission too often and instead of teaching their students how to think critically, they indoctrinate them so that they vote for the same party the teacher does and echo the opinions the teacher expresses in class. Furthermore, some teachers harass students whose opinions they do not like, and even encourage the harassment of students who do not agree with the teacher's political views. Teachers who indoctrinate are especially vicious because besides not respecting pluralism, which is a cornerstone of the democratic system, they abuse the power they have over the students to manipulate them. In authoritarian systems teachers are nothing but instruments of the state to make obedient citizens out of their students.

Glossary

Bribe- to offer money or other gifts to politicians in exchange for favors.

Demagoguery- A political leader who tells the people what they want to hear, independently of whether it is true or not.

Lobbies- representatives of interest groups who can exert pressure on politicians by offering donations to parties.

Organized crime- Groups that operate nationally or internationally in illicit activities, like the illegal sale of drugs, human trafficking, or prostitution.

Political indifference- Apathy regarding political developments.

Terrorist organizations- Groups that use terror with the aim of achieving their (usually political) ends.

Topics for discussion

1. What do you think is the right way of reacting to undemocratic behavior in a democracy?

2. How should a democratic system deal with politicians engaged in corrupt behavior?

Questions

1. What are the characteristics of a demagogue?

____

____

____

____

____

2. Why is ignorance so destructive?

____

____

____

____

____

3. Give two examples of undemocratic behavior.

____

____

____

____

____

4. Think of a powerful lobby that exerts pressure on politicians.

____

____

____

____

5. The United States government announced in September 2020 that both the Antifa movement and the Ku Klux Klan would be declared terrorist organizations. Do you think that the government is right in doing so?

____

____

____

____

6. Give one example of organized crime.

____

____

____

____

7. Do you think that a politically indifferent citizen should complain about government inefficiency?

____

____

____

____

____

8. Should a teacher have the right to express her political views in
    class if she respects the views of her students? Why?

____

____

____

____

____

7. Conclusion: Assuming our rights and obligations as citizens in a democracy

7.1. The right to be yourself

As has been repeatedly expressed in this book, one of the cornerstones of democracy is pluralism, and pluralism is based on tolerance. In a democracy, the citizen has a right to her own views, her own convictions and her own lifestyle. It does not matter what your friends or relatives say about your opinions or your lifestyle: nobody can decide for you.

While minors need the protection of parents or guardians, children have rights in a democracy, and parents who do not respect the rights of their children can lose the custody of their children and/or be prosecuted. In most democracies of the world a person comes of age at 18, and this means that she is free to live her life as she desires.

This includes renouncing a religious faith, adopting a new one, or not having one at all. It includes the right to choose your friends or your partner, without the interference of other people, deciding what profession you want to practice, your place of residence, etc.

7.2. The right to express your views peacefully

In a democracy, everybody has a right to their opinion, and to express it if it is done in a peaceful manner. While freedom of speech is a pillar of democracy, it is an offence to slander people, to incite to violence or to threaten other people. Likewise, while democracy gives us the right to demonstrate for what we believe in, we must do it in a peaceful manner, avoiding damage to property or hurting other people. Those who demonstrate violently, incite to violence or to riots break the law and are prosecuted.

Pluralism implies that people can have ideas that seem unacceptable to other people. However, a democracy does not prohibit ideas; it prohibits behavior that jeopardizes the democratic order: An individual can be against abortion and express her views, but she may not attack patients, doctors or nurses at an abortion clinic. In the same manner, a person can be in favor of abortion, but she may not harass, insult or attack people who are against abortion.

Thus, a person can have "very noble" principles, but if she uses violence to defend those principles, she breaks the law. In contrast, another individual can have ideas that may seem unacceptable to many, but if she expresses them peacefully, she does not break the law.

Another cornerstone of democracy is the equality of all citizens before the law, and this means that the law is applied in the same manner independently of who the citizens are or what convictions they have.

7.3.   The right to a private life

As we saw in chapter 3, in a democracy there is a division between the realms of public and private life. That is not the case neither in authoritarian, nor totalitarian or theocratic systems. The reason is that these systems do not recognize pluralism and expect the citizen to obey the mandates of the state in every aspect, even in their private lives.

In a democracy, the state has nothing to say about how a citizen leads her private life- whether she wants to have a partner (as long as the partner is an adult), the sex of the partner, to have a sex life, or to get married or not. The only limits to how we lead or lives in a democracy are that we respect the laws of the state and the rights of others.

It is illegal to infringe on the private lives of other citizens, like some unethical journalists do. Defamation, that is, injuring the reputation of a person, is punishable by law.

Likewise, in a democracy we are free to join any association or group we want to, without the interference of the state. Exceptions to this rule are of course terrorist organizations, organized crime, and religious sects that limit the freedom of their members, or other groups which do not recognize the rule of law.

7.4.   The obligation to respect the law

While in a democracy citizens are free to lead the lives they wish, they have the obligation of respecting the law. It does not matter if the citizen is a man, a woman, young, old, religious or atheist. The laws apply to all citizens independently of their personal characteristics, and not obeying them results in prosecution and punishment.

One quite common problem of democracies in the 21st century is political polarization. People seem to forget that their political opponents have rights, too. Whilst it is perfectly acceptable to engage in a debate with our opponents, it is not acceptable to insult them, spit on them, beat them up, threaten them or harm them just because we happen to disagree with them.

Likewise, while democratic governments grant us the right to demonstrate, they do NOT grant us the right to riot or to destroy property. If citizens want to demonstrate they have to obtain a permit first and follow what the authorities say. Sometimes the authorities may deny a permit, for example, for reasons of public health. Or the local government may change the place where the demonstration takes place if it can cause traffic problems. If a certain group has obtained a permit for a peaceful demonstration, it is not democratic to counter demonstrate at the same place and at the same time without a permit, just to sabotage the right to demonstrate of others we do not like.

In a state where there is rule of law, we cannot take justice in our own hands, independently of how much others have wronged us. The state has the monopoly of the use of violence through the police, who are the representatives of the law. However, in a democracy police officers who abuse their power can be reported and face harsh consequences, including prosecution and incarceration.

7.5.   The obligation to respect the rights of others

Just as we like to decide for ourselves how we want to live our lives, other people have the same right. If my friend or relative adopts a lifestyle different from, or even conflicting with mine, I have nothing to say if this lifestyle does not break the law.

Other people have the right to express their own opinions and to demonstrate for the causes they believe just. If I do not like their views, I have the right to avoid their company, but not the right to harass them because they do not agree with me.

It is precisely tolerance and pluralism what make life possible for so many different people in a democracy. Not tolerating differences is therefore undemocratic and even dangerous.

7.6.   The right (or obligation) to be informed

While some might argue that information is a right, others regard it as a civil obligation. If we are not informed, we cannot defend our rights, much less hold civil servants accountable for their actions. We have the responsibility to make sure that stories we share with others on social media are neither fake news nor slander.

In a time where the use of social media bots as well as an overabundance of information have become commonplace, the citizen must check if what she is reading is truth or plain fake and assume responsibility for what she publishes.

7.7.   The right (or responsibility) to vote

Opinions are divided on whether voting is a right or a responsibility. As we have seen before, public officials are elected through the suffrage of the electors. In a democracy a politician does not decide whether he stays in power for another mandate- it is the people who express their political will through elections.

In many countries, there are no elections. The people must obey whatever their leaders say. It does not matter whether the leaders represent the people or not. Neither do people have influence on what politicians do. In those regimes, the only alternative people have for a change is to revolt because politicians will not step down, independently of how hated they are.

Thousands of people have sacrificed their lives for democracy, that is, for the right to vote. Yet, due to the nature of democratic systems, people cannot be obliged to vote. The problem is that people who do not vote cannot expect a change either. And as it has been presented before, often the people who would most benefit from a change are the ones less interested in bringing it about.

7.8.   Democracy is a fragile system

It is by far easier to keep order in an authoritarian or totalitarian system than in a democracy. Leaders do not need the approval of the people for doing whatever they wish. Nor are they accountable for human rights violations.

In a democracy, the situation is quite different: politicians have to fulfill their promises if they (or their parties) intend to be reelected. Moreover, politicians have to respect the people, even if some of the people did not vote for them or do not like them. But perhaps the characteristic that makes democracy stand out from other systems of government is **accountability**. Time and again politicians are prosecuted and incarcerated for corruption, or for other crimes as anybody else would be. Politicians are not above the law. In a democracy, nobody's interests come before the law.

Perhaps one of the greatest challenges of democracy is practicing tolerance with intolerant groups or individuals. Democracy rests on pluralism, which is based on tolerance, or the peaceful coexistence of differences. Differences can be striking. People can get to dislike other people to a great degree. But in a democracy, everybody has rights, and the law is above all citizens.

When citizens do not respect law and order, and press the state to use force, their rights are curtailed. A government can announce extraordinary measures or the temporary suspension of civil rights. But it may not break the laws of the state.

Unfortunately, there are many examples in history of democratic states which have turned authoritarian, when the division of powers is not respected, or the rights of opponents are ignored. One example is the Spanish Civil War (1936-1939). The Republican government banned the Falangist party and the Falangists started meeting cladenstinely. They later organized a military coup and overthrew the government. A long period of authoritarian rule followed, and democracy was finally restored in 1975, more than 35 years after the end of the Spanish Civil War.

www.ingramcontent.com/pod-product-compliance
Lightning Source LLC
LaVergne TN
LVHW051123180726
843512LV00012B/917